Praise for
B.V. Olguín's
Red Leather Gloves

I could mess around with these poems all day, just for the pleasure of their music and their richness of story, content, and of course, heart. Lots and lots of heart!

—Kristin Naca, author of *Bird Eating Bird*

Red Leather Gloves achieves the difficult task of making an ancient sport, known for its brutality, worthy of poetic representation through striking and dignified verse that hits hard. A former boxer, Olguín demonstrates an insider's knowledge of the sport, which allows him to avoid sentimental or romantic depictions. These poems are real, beautiful grittiness.

—Carlos Gallego, Ph.D., English Professor and Boxing Club Head Coach, St. Olaf College

This pugilist poet pulls no punches, his poetry flows round to round with graceful jab like precision and never lets up on its intensity. These poems are hard-hitting lessons from the square ring. *Red Leather Gloves* is a solid debut.

—Gregg Barrios, author of *Rancho Pancho* and *La Causa*

A beautiful collection! Each poem in *Red Leather Gloves* is a victory!

—Frances Treviño, author of *Cayetana: Poems*

Poetry is about transcending the subject matter, and *Red Leather Gloves* tells a story of courage, of the human will to survive against all odds and at any cost, of the brutal vulnerability of humanity.

—Richard Blanco, 2013 Presidential Inaugural Poet and author of *Looking for the Gulf Motel*

Olguín brings the reader right into the ring, into his barrio Magnolia, into the Olympiad, with language that is direct and so vivid that at times I swear I can smell the smells. These poems are so gripping a reader will be forever changed.

—Wendy Barker, Ph.D., author of *Nothing Between Us*

Red Leather Gloves

Red Leather Gloves

Poems by

B.V. Olguín

HANSEN PUBLISHING GROUP

Red Leather Gloves
Copyright © 2014 by B.V. Olguín

ISBN: (PAPER) 978-1-60182-058-7
ISBN: (EBOOK) 978-1-60182-061-7

Cover design and book interior design by Jon Hansen

Hansen Publishing Group, LLC
302 Ryders Lane
East Brunswick, NJ 08816

http://hansenpublishing.com

for Kino
whose greatest victory
was never learning the lessons we were taught in the ring

y

pa' mis tíos Valdez
who had no choice but to perfect them

Boxing has become America's tragic theater.

—Joyce Carol Oates, *On Boxing* (1987)

Contents

Acknowledgments xi

I. RED LEATHER GLOVES
Teeth 3
The Weigh-In 4
Red Leather Gloves 5
Knockout 6
In This Corner 8
The Olympiad 9
Gallos 10
Gold 11
Fingers 13
Boys 14

II. BOXING LESSONS & BODY SHOTS
Madrina 17
Balls 19
Legs 21
Stomach 23
Killer Instinct 25
Jab 27
Double Right Cross 29
Tournament 31
Taboo 33
Mercy 34

III. THE SWEET SCIENCE
Mouse 39
Chin 41
Skull 43
Noses 45
Face 46
The Beast 47
The Sweet Science 48
Strange Fruit 50
The Ring 52
Ars Poetica 54

IV. GLADIATORS

Work 57

Gladiator 59

Ode to the Bronx Everlast Factory, 1917-2003 61

Sign of the Cross 64

The Kid from Magnolia...66

Pascal's Wager 68

Man to Man...71

Prettyboy 73

The Docks..75

Catfight...77

Pound For Pound..79

My Tía Lucy Hates Boxing 82

Twist..85

V. ODE TO ALI

Ode to Ali 89

Glossary...93

Boxing Weight Divisions..95

About the Author 96

ACKNOWLEDGMENTS

I am indebted to Sandra Cisneros and members of the Macondo Writers Workshop for their support and assistance on this book. I am especially grateful to Richard Blanco and Ruth Behar for facilitating the master poetry workshop that helped me turn a series of cathartic poems into a book length meditation on the salience of violence in my life and in contemporary society. Vicente Lozano, Luís Rodriguez and additional members of our 2005 workshop provided honest critiques of early versions of these poems. Richard Blanco, Gregorio Barrios and Wendy Barker provided indispensable suggestions on the first complete draft of the collection. My compañera Bernadette Andrea provided insights and encouragement necessary to bring this project to completion. Jon Hansen was visionary, gracious, and patient with my angst-ridden return to the painful part of my life and was an expert steward in the larger effort required to get this book to the public. ¡Muchísimas gracias a todos!

Earlier versions of poems from this manuscript are reprinted with permission of the following journals: "Chin," *North American Review* (Finalist, 2008 James Hearst Poetry Prize); "The Olympiad," *Callaloo* (2008); and "The Docks," *Callaloo* (2008).

I also greatly appreciate the recognition that earlier versions of this manuscript received from the following presses:

First Runner Up, 2007 Kent State Wick Poetry Center Manuscript Prize;
Finalist, 2007 & 2008 Marsh Hawk Press Poetry Manuscript Prize;
Finalist, 2008 May Swenson Poetry Manuscript Award;
Semi-Finalist, 2008 Elixir Press Poetry Manuscript Award;
Semi-Finalist, 2008 & 2012 Notre Dame Andrés Montoya Poetry Prize.

Epigraphs for the book parts and individual poems are cited from the following sources:

Introduction (p. iv), Adolf Hitler, *Mein Kampf*, Vol. II [1926] (Embassy 2005)
Introduction (p. iv), Joyce Carol Oates, *On Boxing* [1989] (Harper 2006)

Part 1 (p. 1), Virgil, *Aeneid*, Book 5, lines 537-49, Trans. John Dryden
  (Penguin 1997)
Part 2 (p. 15), Joyce Carol Oates, *On Boxing* [1989] (Harper 2006)
"Killer Instinct" (p. 25), Thomas Hobbes, *Leviathan* [1651] (Empire 2013)
"Killer Instinct" (p. 25), Karl Marx, *Sixth Thesis on Feuerbach* [1845], in
  Collected Works of Karl Marx & Friedrich Engels, Vol. 5 (International
  Publishers 1976)
Part 3 (p. 37), Homer, *The Iliad*, Book 23, Trans. Samuel Butler (El Paso
  Norte 2006)
"Strange Fruit" (p. 50), "Strange Fruit," by Abel Meeropol (1937), sung
  by Billie Holiday (1939), Public Domain
"The Ring" (p. 52), Mike Tyson, Public Domain
Part 4 (p. 55), Marlon Brando, *On The Waterfront* [1954], Dir. Elia Kazan
  (Sony 2001)
"Gladiator" (p. 59), Pindar, *The Odes*, 476 BCE, Trans. G.S. Conway
  (Orion 1998)
"Gladiator" (p. 59), Chant at Roman Gladiator Fights, circa. 100 CE
"Pascal's Wager" (p. 68), Blaise Pascal, *Pensées and Other Writings* [1650],
  Trans. Honor Levi (Oxford 2008)
"Man to Man" (p. 71), Emile Griffith in Ron Ross, *Nine...Ten...and Out:
  The Two Worlds of Emile Griffith* (DiBella, 2008)
"Catfight" (p. 77), Joyce Carol Oates, *On Boxing* [1987] (Harper 2006)
Part 5 (p. 87), Muhammad Ali (1963)

I.

RED LEATHER GLOVES

With fear and wonder seiz'd, the crowd beholds
The gloves of death, with sev'n distinguish'd folds
Of tough bull hides; the space within is spread
With iron, or with loads of heavy lead:
Darés himself was daunted at the sight,
Renounc'd his challenge, and refus'd to fight.
Astonish'd at their weight, the hero stands,
And pois'd the pond'rous engines in his hands.
"What had your wonder," said Entellus, "been,
Had you the gauntlets of Alcides seen,
Or view'd the stern debate on this unhappy green!
These which I bear your brother Eryx bore,
Still mark'd with batter'd brains and mingled gore."

—Virgil, *Aeneid*, Book 5 (lines 537-49)

TEETH

Coach Jim means well, I know, just worries
I'll lose a filling in the chipped front tooth
that still held after five years and a month
of training for my first fight. Welfare medicine

is not supposed to be this good. He pulls my lip up
slow from the corner, curious like a pimp
lifts the dress of a runaway. He grabs my tooth
between knuckle and thumb, pulls back and forth,

back and forth with the full weight of his body
refusing to accept defeat by strange composites
of dental cement: *I'm afraid you're gonna lose it in the ring,*
he assures with the calculated cadence of a doctor

who can think of no more medicines to prescribe.
His other thumb fondles the bottom lip, pushing
at my gums for no apparent reason. Then the nose.
He smashes sharp bones in my cheeks

with his palms, waiting for a grimace, looking
for tears, wondering with his hands if I am worth
the time, how many teeth I am willing to lose, how much
I care about my nose, the shape of my face,

how much of myself I am willing to surrender.

THE WEIGH-IN

He isn't a real doctor, Kino says, but
the pot-bellied man fondles
the scale's long metal arm
as if his fat fingered tap of the weight

will somehow heal us. He snorts
short pig grunts each time he pokes
the scope light into a new hole
because he knows he's center stage. This

is boxing; the weigh-in an opening act
of a Greek tragedy with a cast of characters
who won't know if they are villains or victims
until long after they have lined up naked

like a row of bodies at auction. I'm next.
The floating foot-stand slips as if to say
something is wrong with so many men watching
the finger tap rhythm increasing and

decreasing my number, the rod bouncing
up and down like a fighter
losing control of his legs. *Stand still
and drop 'em.* I do, wide-eyed wondering

how much white cotton underwear can weigh;
as everyone watches my balls wrinkle and shrink
like a novice will do before his first fight
until he finds out a punch doesn't hurt

right away. My arms. Where are my arms?
The bell? Why doesn't it just ring already
so I can let loose on one of the other boys
lined up behind me, pants down, waiting

their turn to be picked and poked
with cold things that will turn us all
into animals in the ring…

RED LEATHER GLOVES

After fighting to shake off red leather gloves
into another boy's face, the pain comes back again
because your hands are wrapped too tight, so tight
it hurts to stay still. This is why you hit so hard.

There is nothing more to do but wait,
arms at your side silent, head down, determined
to decipher the mathematical formula
that keeps shoelaces from coming undone.

Your father unties each glove, one hole at a time.
Laces are getting too expensive to cut off
like they do on TV. And another boy
needs them for the next fight. So you wait,

just wait, trying to unlock the logic of laces,
why they take so long to undo, why
gloves hurt so much except when you hit
something, someone, anyone.

Your eyes mapping miniature rivers
flowing down forearms. New veins
of dried up tears sprout everywhere and
sweat beads crawl across the mountain range

of goose bumps that rise after every fight
because the AC is always too high
and these gypsy arenas never have more
than a hole in the wall to vent

smoke from other fathers waiting
to noose red leather gloves onto sons, tight,
so tight their arms will flail like a stabbed fish
trying to break loose.

KNOCKOUT

After arms stop churning champagne bubbles
from his crooked jaw, you recognize them
as your own again. They grow from chest
to heart-shaped leather sacks
that are supposed to keep fists
from drawing blood.

He tries to back away but the ropes
won't let him. You've got him now,
your left forearm forming the straight back
of a bloodhound on a scent
as he hides behind hands

pressed hard to mouth, trying
to keep that primal scream from escaping
through padded gloves turned to rock,
boulders, a mountain
too large and heavy to hold.

His frozen eyeballs push their way
through tightened slits, floating
in a puddle of scarlet and white
and some strange glowing yellow
that seems to say: *you did this.*

And you want to reach over,
just reach over, throw your arms
around his neck like you have been trained
to do when hurt. But this
would be a real hug, awkward
with gloves, but a hug nonetheless.

You want to squeeze him tight, chest to chest
like your mother did when you saw *el cuquí;*
hold him, kiss his forehead
with your boxer's big bruised lips
so he knows you will protect him
from evil only children see.

But you can't. They won't let you.
If you let him recover they will hate you,
call you *Stupid Meskin. Pussy. Maricón.*
Dark-skinned men with flat noses like your uncles
will whistle that rhythmic curse:
¡Chin-ga-tú-maaa-dre Pu-to!

You know they have paid hard earned cash
to see boys broken, so you let go
of your arms again, ashamed
of what they are about to do.

IN THIS CORNER

Money's on red tonight, big money, even some twenties
wagered in whispers on a one hundred six pound *Maskin boy*
who made weight 'cause his daddy couldn't find work this week.
They know what they're doing; can read boxing trunks
like a pensioner sizes up a horse's butt at the track.

This one wears white cotton gym shorts thin as underwear
from a Sears clearance aisle and dirty Converse high tops
that smile from the back because the rubber sole
couldn't help but come undone after a year of beatings.
Money's on red 'cause the boy's got no socks

and the announcer says something about *Magnolia*,
The Kid from Magnolia. More whispers wet with whiskey
from beneath bleachers until someone turns a belch
into a gurgling *grito* that unleashes whistling and catcalls,
a symphony of rising baritone taunts for the ref

to stop mumbling and set them loose already:
the black boy in that corner, the Mexican in this one,
staring wide-eyed at each other's burnt toast skin
that has attracted a flock of fluttering seagulls fighting
each other's squawks for the right to take the first bite.

THE OLYMPIAD

This is that crumbling red brick building
where commodities were sold in shouts
not so long ago people still remember the sound
of fortunes being made on a fistful of cotton
pulled from life by dark and dirty field hands.

This is where we fight for the right to eat;
the wet wooden stairwell winding us up
to a second floor gallows, gutted now
but for water-stained fight posters
of so many men who look alike
because they all have the same violent father.

And the ring: four ceiling posts
strung with hairy hemp rope that can cut
a crooked smile across a man's back
if he dares stop swinging. The Olympiad,
corner of Congress and Main Street

in downtown Houston, where Darryl Brumley
told the world he would one day be champ
only to be shot in the gut a few days later.
He should have known better
than to walk around here at night.

This is that crumbling red brick building
where carloads of brown boys, black boys and
men the color of bruises cue up, anxious
to pick and pull at each other
in hope of escaping the welfare line,

even though they suspect this is where it begins.
The Olympiad; its long line of dark bodies swinging,
limbs twitching to get started, yet
secretly hoping someday, someone
will tear this thing down.

GALLOS

His black rag of curls pulled into a fluffy pillow
by the other boy who never learned to snap elbows
so punches landed flush; both wailing arms
like a wounded bird flutters to keep control
after being shot in mid-flight.

They lash each other with roundhouse lace slaps
as if hurling rocks, sticks, broken bottles.
One tries to knee the other in the balls, pull him down
with a headlock, mount him like a stallion
does a broken mare until the ref breaks in again.

Two weeks of training never took hold
because it wasn't enough to begin with.
But no one cares who wins. Pure gambling.
All we know is one wounded *gallo*
will back into the rope noose

of the boy who flails the most, the boy
who doesn't care about bets on the side
or free hotdogs for fighters. He knows
this is for real, so real he'll swing
at the ref for getting in the way.

The winner will be the red-eyed boy
who spits out his mouthpiece
like a soldier does a hand grenade pin
before charging, head down, all arms alive
as red leather gloves splatter all over his gut.

GOLD

Kino sniffed gold spray paint
from a red bandana every afternoon
we waited for a bus to the gym
twenty miles away, past docks and
cracked streets coach Jim called *Coontown*.

It wasn't far enough for Kino
to recover from aerosol
dreams he'd somehow
make the Olympic team.
He's the one who started me boxing

because I believed his heavy-breathed hype
we'd both win gold medals
even though I knew he was no good
at throwing punches. And
he panicked when hit

because the flash focused everything
too fast. He couldn't take the jolts
that made the ring bolts rattle like a ball bearing
trying to break out of a can. Huffing
helped, but Kino's hands were so slowed

by the sprayed cotton rag
they looked like torn sails fluttering
to fight off the gloved gale storm
of another boy. Kino sprayed
golden wet flakes of paint into a rag

until they puddled and stunk
so much his eyes lacquered
like that Olympian whose legs shook
on the podium when he raised the gold
to his lips as the colored flag unfurled

and his song was sung. Kino
never won a fight. The last time
coach Jim took a chance
he pitched the towel in the first round
straight into Kino's face and

screamed, *This ain't swimmin'!*
when he saw Kino couldn't keep afloat
no matter how much he wound
his rotary arms to keep from drowning
in midair.

FINGERS

These things I carry, small and thin
as a girl's nails would snap broken
if not for tight white Everlast wraps.
They were never meant to crack
the hard shell of a forehead. Fingers
fisted into drill bits

forced to dig for crimson crude
in the sea beneath another boy's face.
Whole hands made hard as metal
because coach Jim made me soak them
in boiling salt water an hour a day
so they swelled into weapons
to crush bones like Autumn leaves
underfoot.

At fifteen my dumbbell hands hang
heavy at the side, too clunky to hold a girl,
squeeze her to me, tickle
the small of her back until we giggle
so much we forget to kiss.

BOYS

Everyone aims below the belt
in church basement dressing rooms
where we change into a rainbow
of shorts that will make us men.
Still hairless, curious,

we can't figure out
how something so small
as a *chile*-shaped *verga*
can determine our fate
in the ring.

Coach Jim says
you can judge a fighter
by his balls: *big balls*
means you're brave; a big
dick makes you mean as a bull.

How can we not stare
at the one place
we aren't allowed to feel
with our fists? Coaches
stare, too, pretending not

to notice naked brown bodies
as they take their time
threading each glove hole
with a lacetip squeeze
they moisten with spit.

II.

BOXING

LESSONS &

BODY SHOTS

Boxing is a celebration of the lost religion of masculinity all the more trenchant for its being lost. —Joyce Carol Oates, *On Boxing* (1989)

MADRINA

The same soft hands that wound
first communion beads around my fist
unfolded the middle finger
with a whisper: *Fuck you.*
Tell him fuck you.

This would be my first fight:
your neighbor's son.
The pat on my back forcing feet
forward in a slow sliding shuffle
as you had done in church
weeks before; my finger

flipped out, hand waving up,
down and to the sides mouthing
Fuck you! Fuck you! Fuck you!
as if this were another rote recitation
from Catechism class.
Madrina Lola, Tía Dolores,

you taught me your name
means *pains* in Spanish, *many pains*,
when I was ten and a half.
A boy must learn these things
while there still is time
for lessons to take hold.

This is what a godmother is for:
to teach a boy how to shoot the finger,
twist a belt around the fist, swing
it horsewhip quick so silver buckle snaps
into the shallow soft back
of another ten-year-old boy

taught to do the same to me.
Like an obedient alter boy swaying
a weighted metal incense can at mass

17

I swung my coiled brown strap
until the snap and punching bag thud
said *UGHT!* like a Medieval monk

whipping off sticky pink slices
of evil skin, one lash at a time,
or a husband beating his wife
with a slick leather belt in grunts
that push it all up from the groin:
UGHT! UGHT! UGHT!

He held it in as long as he could
but the choir in his throat
couldn't stay silent after the priest
broke the wafer and said:
This is my body, the body of Christ,
that was given up for you...

His solo aria bringing both families
to their feet, face to face, fingers
flaring and shouts loud as prayer
and cheers from the bleachers.

BALLS

Balls, coach Jim says, fingering
faded Wrangler blue jeans
always too big for him
to get a good hold.

It all comes down to balls,
you know, Boe-lahs,
he whispers his best
whiskey Spanish.

So I go down
with a crooked hook
when the ref ain't lookin',
then up quick to hide my crime.

If he gets up I'll shoot again,
feeling with fists for soft spots
between legs, kidneys
or under arm pits

if he's careless
enough to think
he can protect his face
without paying a price.

I'll swing hard and fast
so fast punches blur into one
as if plated in place
like a plastic gold trophy.

A golden boy never stops
swinging because he knows
how an empty stomach howls
and how leather hits hurt

inside out with a dull thud:
a loaf of bread falling to the floor
at the grocery store, a pouch
of rice, ten pound bag of sugar

trying not to burst from its own weight,
a rack of beans broken,
whole shelves thundering undone
if you drop your hands.

So I aim for the head,
belly, the balls because
I know Coach Jim bet
a hundred dollars on me;

I fear the gut-growling shame
of standing center ring
with hand held down by the ref;
and I want to eat tonight.

LEGS

Tonight's lesson was legs:
Watch his legs! Legs!
Watch his legs!
was all coach Jim could shout

to avoid the fact
his fighter was going down
a third time in two rounds.
Dance! G'dammit! Dance!

Shooting his head left then right
to wash off another fighter
who let him down
like he always knew they would.

There was still a lesson
in all this: *Toes.*
On your toes,
gotta use your toes, boys...

He paused to remember
what came next, searching
for the right word
but settling for *legs* again,

spelling each letter
with a torn glove grin
as he hooked his head left
like a punch line

to the tall ring girl
in a black bikini
who had forced a smile,
when her high heel

caught the rope
as she tried to tip toe
out the ring
between rounds.

STOMACH

Fans don't know about the hunger.
A boxer is hungry, always
hungry, afraid an extra pound
will force him to face a fighter
one division up, broader shoulders
and a square jaw crunching air before the bell
as if it were food.

A boxer is thirsty, too, because coach
will make him run the arena
on fight day to make weight,
then force him to spit
in a Coke can all afternoon
until his tongue turns to cardboard
for just a quarter pound.

He was always hungry.
Free lunch at school a reminder
his stomach still felt empty
even after the apple he stole
when no one was looking. And
there was never enough stringy *fideo*
and pork bones because food stamps
always run out before the end of the month.

He remembers *tortillas* every day,
and *pan dulce* coach won't let him eat
because of all the *manteca*.
A boxer dreams of food
he never ate: filet mignon
wrapped in bacon, baked potatoes
with cheese, sour cream and
more bacon on top
like the commercial. He stares

at the sea beyond ropes,
wondering about lobster
and strange purple fish eggs
hatching in rich people's stomachs.
He dreams of food between each round
of sparring; the feast he'll fund with winnings
from the weekend fight. Food,
and champagne, too,
if he can just make weight.

Every day in the gym tracking
the man in the mirror, bobbing and
weaving like an ancient tribesman
preparing for the hunt. He rifles
arms into mitts to make sure
his aim is right; hits
speed bag with rapid-fire fists staclattering
like hunters felling whole herds;
he grabs the heavy bag
as if it were a fat rack of marbled meat.

Each mile of roadwork
will someday earn a big bowl
of fancy spaghetti; two hundred sit ups a day
dig furrows across his stomach
that front row fans see as beautiful.

KILLER INSTINCT

Bellum omnium contra omnes.
—Thomas Hobbes, Leviathan (1651)

But the human essence is no abstraction inherent in each single individual. In its reality it is the ensemble of social relations.
—Karl Marx, Sixth Thesis on Feuerbach (1845)

Men in the family proud
I could pull a pint of blood
without crying from cuts
or losing control
like a wounded wolf cub.
Eyes alive sniffing

every pawed step
'cause everybody's got friends
and they'd get you sooner or later
if you shuffled too fast or
too slow down schoolhouse halls
and barrio street gauntlets.

Killer instinct, dad said once
and sent me hunting
anyone who started a rumor,
egged our house or
carried the ball on the field.

Coach Hill called me *headhunter*,
engraved my name on a trophy
the same week I got suspended
for fighting. A father's pride.
Tío Nick, too.

Our family's best boxer
crowned me *street fighter*
for what I had done
at Navarro's Food Mart,
Mexican Park the week before,
and the washateria.

Coach Jim called it natural talent
and planned to make me pro
as soon as I turned seventeen
'cause he said, *you're getting too damn good
to keep fightin' for free.*

Sniffing every scuffed step
down Edison Junior High halls,
stoned from the morning joint because
Robert Castillo was getting linemen
from my own team to jump me

for blackening his eye in the showers,
and Michael Sears was still pissed
from the fight last year.
He knew enough enemies
to set an ambush after math class.

My whole body a blade,
fists serrated by rote routines
and advice from older men
who haven't forgotten
their own childhood enemies,
and are still trying to gather a gang
to get 'em after the bell rings.

JAB

Old timers say you can win a fight
with just a jab. And this is true
as any religion. If a boy believes
long enough, hard enough,
hits will flow like faith, natural
as a palm frond flipping and flapping
after each gust of hurricane hail.

A jab should be trapdoor quick
but rubbery enough to bounce a fistball
against the wall of another boy's face
over and over again and again
until the wall gives up
or the ball.

An old timer will tell you
no one ever became champ
without first learning to step
into left-handed slapshots
then back and side to side
without missing a beat so punches
run together like a machine gun burst
used to spring an army ambush.

If you learn your lesson well
no fighter will get within four feet
for fear of what you can do
with the left twisting wrist flick
and fist that will shock
like a woman's slap
long enough to hide
a right cross canon blast
that'll make the whole ring recoil.

Old timers say a well-learned jab
will follow you forever. And this is true:
once an elbow is cocked

it can fire on its own and
neither a smile nor open-handed offer
will escape the gun-barrel shine
in your right eye or
twitching trigger finger elbow
that will keep anyone, everyone,
from getting too close.

DOUBLE RIGHT CROSS

The double right cross
is designed to scramble brains
by sneaking in and out
like a silent thief who knows
he's doing something wrong.

This isn't just any punch.
You save it for last
like a too sweet desert
that'll make a boy break out in hives
as soon as cherry red leather gloves
touch his lips.

But you've gotta set him up.
The double right cross takes time
if its gonna work
without setting you up
for a counterpunch combo
that'll paint your face
all the silly colors of a clown.

It can take a whole night
of close dancing and fondling
his face with left fist slaps
before he gets distracted enough
to slip step into range
and drop his left guard to paw
away the nuisance
that'll leave him open.

The worst thing you can do
is open up too soon and miss
so the wind whispers a warning
the killer is loose. This
will make him close up too tight
for you to stick it in.

It can take a whole night
before he lowers his left
long enough for you to double up.
And it won't work
if you don't double up;
the physics of fists all backwards:

force comes from energy
used to pull the right fist back
in place with a snap so fast
you punch yourself in the face.
You double a right cross
to land just one punch.

It's the first blow that counts.
That's the secret. You double up
so the first shot flings
back so fast the fist floats
like the tail tip of a leather whip,
weightless for a split second
before flipping up at the end of its sling
to become a wrecking ball.

The second punch won't hit anything
if the first is flung out fast and far
as if you were disowning part of yourself
long enough for it to commit the crime
but too quick for anyone to notice
until the body is found
lying on the padded canvas ground.

TOURNAMENT

Knock this niggah out, coach Jim hissed
as if still spitting blood
through the face slit cut
by another coach last tournament
where so many sucker punch chairs flew
the ref called the fight
with two minutes to go.

A wager gone wrong? A word?
He whispered it again
trying to muster enough courage
to fight the boy himself,
winding my laces an hour early
to make me desperate to shake them off
into soothing black skin.

Niggahs cheat, coach Jim always says,
so when the ref stopped the clock
to grab his spit mouthpiece,
coach Jim jumped the ring and
refused to back down
'til the ref threatened
to disqualify me.

It happened again in round two;
in the third he just couldn't take it:
NIGGAH STOP CHEATIN'!
The crowd was with him,
on their feet, beer cups cooling us off
with warm vinegar stench.

And then it started:
Niggah! Mayate! FUCKIN' COON!
Each voice clanging against the other
like a group of musicians warming instruments
that can't help but sound different
as they play the same song.

The ref stopped the fight five full minutes,
arms out in a cross, palms flapping
down, down, down like a conductor
who has lost control of the horn section,
his body slipping between us
so we wouldn't succumb to training
and start swinging again, his face
pivoting on a strained neck muscle

like a wounded bird searching
for the source, wishing
he could go back to the beginning,
or just stop this thing forever,
end the nonsense that makes men mean,
cut off gloves and force us to shake hands,
give us both a trophy and a dollar each
for popcorn and strawberry sodas.

But this was boxing. And he knew better.

TABOO

For Ray "Boom Boom" Mancini
In Memory of Duk Koo Kim, killed in the ring November 13, 1982

He walks in the gym one month later, slow
shifting foot to foot like a punch drunk fighter,
eyes dancing left to right, bobbing and
weaving through the warehouse
of hanging heavy bags and dark-skinned boxers
banging away like murderers.

He is the newest member in that fraternity
of fighters who have killed a man in the ring
and his first day back is awkward as a clinch
because he knows everyone is looking, listening,
searching for the secret in the way his gloves
slap leather mitts.

No one mentions the dead fighter. Ever.
His best stablemate will only say *fuckin' ref, huh,*
expecting no answer as he works speed bag
with hands and feet feeling for an invisible ladder.
Veterans pretend not to notice how he holds back
the overhand right as if it were made of glass.

They know he is useless now and jab stares
across the gym, wagering how many weeks
it will take for him to realize this, too,
and stop coming forever. But
as long as he pretends
to be just another fighter,

little boy boxers will bang away at heavy bags,
meticulously mimicking each apologetic punch,
ignoring knife cut stings into their wrists and
howls from hollow guts with nothing left to vomit
as they force themselves to find
the desire to kill a playmate.

MERCY

Coach Jim made me do it.
Beat tha shit outta'm!
was his favorite phrase
but this time he hissed *ya hear!*
heaving his head

for me to climb the ring
with the bubble-faced white boy
who'd been peeking in the gym
every day for two weeks
before daring to walk all the way in.

Coach Jim was always complaining
about *wets* and *niggahs* but
this boy was pink like him,
from around here, too, poor
like all of us.

Did he see a secret signal
in folds of lingering baby fat
that said this boy
would never be
a champion?

Maybe the sticky wet stink
from dockside refineries,
six colors of peeling paint,
duct-taped heavy bags,
ripped red leather gloves

and still torn canvas
in the far side of the ring
made coach Jim realize
none of us were champions
and never would be. We

were fifty-dollar fighters
who took a match on a day notice
because it was better
than getting beaten for free;
amateurs like Kino

certain he'd make the Olympic team
even though he'd never won a fight.
Maybe coach Jim could see
in this boy's dimpled smile
he'd never taken a punch.

So he set my leash loose,
made me bite with three jabs
and a right cross
twisting and snapping back
like lightning

to make him jump for cover
from that fear of finding out
how pillow soft foam of a glove
can turn to rock in mid-air.

Every fighter knew the ritual:
their side glance glares
returning to bag routines,
jump ropes and the bob and weave
clothesline coach Jim hung up

in front of the garage door
like a policeman's yellow tape
warning a crime
had just been committed here.

Coach Jim was right, after all,
because the boy took a fall
without firing a shot. And

he cried, and kept crying
as he limped out laces,

hiccupping around the maze
of heavy bag stares
straight through the clothesline
and out the double door
forever.

Every fighter turned away,
embarrassed to do anything
but continue punching.
Coach Jim just fumbling crooked fingers
to unleash my laces as fast as he could,

frustrated he still could not afford
fancy new gloves with Velcro.
His husky whiskey wheezing and
frantic folding fingers
signing an apology,

as if trying to explain this boy
wasn't gonna listen to a lecture
'bout staying in school, not drinking,
leaving this dockside dungeon
to build a life somewhere,

anywhere but here,
find a job that'll give him a uniform,
meet a woman, raise a family
and forget any dreams
of ever becoming more
than just working class.

Maybe coach Jim made me break this boy
right then and there out of mercy
and *beat tha shit outta'm*
was all he could say
to keep from crying.

III.

THE SWEET SCIENCE

First he put a waistband round him and then he gave him some well-cut thongs of ox-hide; the two men being now girt went into the middle of the ring, and immediately fell to; heavily indeed did they punish one another and lay about them with their brawny fists. One could hear the horrid crashing of their jaws, and they sweated from every pore of their skin.

—Homer, *The Iliad*, Book 23

MOUSE

You can never predict which padded pat
will pull a bruised ball of blood
under eye socket skin: the mouse.
All boxers get one sooner or later,
a small lump under lower eyelid
rising like a rodent coaxed from its crack
by rattling clacks of a broom stick.

You can never predict where it will run
once burst, but blood always settles
under eyes, darkened and dumb
like a squeezed tube of cheap magenta
turning purple overnight. It hardens
raccoon rouge because the blood
has got nowhere else to go.

Caught one in the ring once:
a quick snapshot that didn't even hurt,
a missed punch, really, rolling off
to cost my stablemate
a double overhand right in return.
But the mump metastasized
like a volcano cap under pressure

from magma disturbed from sleep;
the biology of a mouse as strange
and scientific as subterraneous veins
moving molten mucous rock
through locks and levees that finally break
down in a chain reaction release
that always comes as a surprise.

You never know when it will happen,
or why, or what punch will pull it out
the magician's hat that is your face,
flattened now after so many tricks
before so many people who paid

to see you pull a pigeon or rabbit
or river of scarlet wet ribbon
from the face of the boy
who just maimed yours.

CHIN

Sportscasters don't know shit
about the science of chins.
They've got it all wrong.
There is no such thing
as a *glass chin* or *iron jaw,*
just a fighter who gets caught
by a crooked angled shot
that stretches invisible fault lines
beneath the scalp
until they crack and shake too much
for him to stand up straight.

Every fighter will fall with just a peck
of leather if the kiss is placed right.
It's a simple fact of physics: a fluid-
filled ear crevice keeps every fighter
upright until the leveling rod bubble
is shocked from silent sleep.
It could be a simple six degree jolt up
or down that makes a mind move mad
in search of the symmetry
shaken by a dew drop dripple
or iceberg boulder splash.
It could be anything
because it doesn't take much
to pull a fighter off center.

This is the truth: every fighter
floats on his chin and the best place
to put his brain in a spin
is the lower left tip of the jawbone jut
with a crooked cut up
that can't figure out if it is a hook
or uppercut or just a simple jab.
One padded pat placed right
and the whole thing will sink
like a cheap Mexican puppet

with too few strings to keep working
after one is snapped away by a careless boy
who will be shocked back onto both heels
that everything could fall apart
with such a light touch.

SKULL

It takes skill to crack a man's skull.
You've got to angle hook to head
exactly one inch above the ear
where cranium connects to sidewall bones
by a few flimsy membranes

along fissures of birth
that never really heal.
Strike it right and the skull
will crack like a coconut,
its juicy fruit running out the ear.

Most fighters go straight for the face.
Others attack foreheads
until their wrists swell and knuckles snap
because even a tightly wound fist
can't hold up against solid bone.

The skull never gives up without a fight:
it will bob and bend at the base
then shoot back with a head butt snap
like the wet towel schoolboys use
to torture each other.

It takes patience, one punch
at a time, each headshot
bouncing the brain
like a deformed tennis ball
trying to break out of the ring.

Tiny capillaries cry blood. Cracks
accumulate. You can be sure of this:
after the shouting lights and
prize money that was never enough,
bleached blonds with fake names,

page seven write-up in the sports section,
dropped biceps seven years later,
and blue uniform given all fighters
once they finally realize the pay
isn't worth so much pain,

a boxer will be laid out
on a grey metal gurney
with holes all over for blood to drain.
A man in lab coat with a fancy little saw
buzzing from side to side
like a champion warming up

will make an uppercut
along the skullcap rim
at just the right place
so brains spill out
like waterlogged spaghetti
and too much sauce.

He'll jerk his head
as if slipping a punch
to whisper *subdural hematoma*
before scooping everything
into a plastic red bucket
that gets emptied four times a day.

NOSES

Flattened badges, burnished brown
insignia from an army of thugs
who worship crescent scars above men's eyes.
Withered remnants of a Sephardic past
or bronze pyramids forgotten
so many centuries ago another broken bone
didn't matter. A family

of broken bones: the nose Basilio Ruiz
could rattle like maracas celebrating
another win by *El Huracán del Norte.*
Tío Nick—the Man With the Golden Arm—
could squeeze and twist his upward
so he almost looked European
despite prison-burned brown body.

But uncle Johnny could never get it right:
at sixty he still smiles like a Mexican movie star.
They always have a full set of teeth
and straight noses. My own, sharp and thin
because I never turned pro, betraying
a family of fighters with noses so flat
a bookie could take one look and set a spread
that would make him rich for a day.

FACE
For Ali

Maybe there is something to the shape of a face
after all. Yes. But science has got it all wrong
since Darwin and *Mein Kampf*. Skin hues
have no value. There is no hidden meaning
behind the formula of refracted light. The slope
of a kneaded forehead does not reveal anything
about a brain because we can't understand the circuits
even after cutting the globe open to test the pulp.
No. Those bony brows and misshapen skullcaps
are not vestiges of the humanoid's balancing act
from four feet to two. The rattle of broken nose bones
has no religion or reason like the rituals
of a primitive species that has yet to discover writing.
The slippery slurred speech does not imply simian
ancestry or a new language to a missing link. No.
None of this is true. The shape of a face is too simple
and insignificant to be anything but a symptom
of a society that has made sport of deforming faces
of men who will age into a new race of beings
that can't talk or walk like humans should.

THE BEAST

I saw it face-to-face in the gym once
as I trained for my first fight: the beast
who came on a right cross to the jaw.
It shook the ocean in my ears

off its axis, sent my feet surfing
padded canvas waves of the ring
because the whole thing shook like a skiff
in a wicked hurricane; that storm

all boxers try to outrun; the wicked thing
that makes you hug another man
in front of everyone even though he
is trying to kill you; the beast

who pulls your eyes out
so you see everything and nothing.
It makes you scratch your gloves
inside out like a trapped raccoon clawing

up a tree to escape open mouths
of hounds. By this point
it is always too late to turn off
the iridescent black white light

that catches your tongue like a nightmare,
and makes you mute and dumb and
blind to the thudding windmill sails
that carry you away.

THE SWEET SCIENCE

I know an old timer who'll tell you secrets
of survival in the ring; that ancient science
of bloodletting written in winding recipes
of raised scars across his face.

He gets right to the point.
Doesn't bother with boxing skills or drills
designed to make you punch right
cause he's seen the beast up close
and knows what works and doesn't.

He'll show you how to miss on purpose
so laces slash eyelids that cry blinding blood.
He'll teach you how journeymen head butt
in a hug; how to bite an ear
in a clench so the ref can't see. This
is how fights were won in the old days.

If you listen closely you'll learn
how to poke a pinhole in gloves
so they cut like a barbed wire whip with just a snap.
He'll teach you the role of chin stubble
in days when there was no time limit and
a fighter's fortune was measured in buckets of blood.

If he sees the promise of a pro
he'll reveal the ancient alchemy of recipes
and remedies he learned on the road:
powders placed on gloves to blind a man
one full minute or make him suffocate
when he tries to breathe between rounds.

He'll teach you how to mix a pink potion
to swell a face fat like a circus freak
with nothing more than a pat. And he knows
the right temperature to cook nitroglycerines
to hold you up when you can't feel your feet.

He has a magic liquid mixed with turpentine
that makes cuts forget to bleed;
an invisible gel that forces fists to slide off
your face like an unintended kiss.

If you pay attention, he'll teach you
how to inhale composites of camphor oil
and gasoline to clear crushed cartilage
so you can make it to the final bell
without drowning in snot.

He knows all these things, this old timer
with a memory like a Medieval torture manual
filled with strange secrets of science
made by men who might be
true doctors or priests or philosophers
if not for all the madness.

STRANGE FRUIT
For Ronnie Shields

> *Southern trees bear a strange fruit:*
> *blood on the leaves and blood on the root;*
> *black bodies swinging in the southern breeze;*
> *strange fruit hanging from the poplar trees*
>
> — "Strange Fruit," by Abel Meeropol (1937),
> sung by Billie Holiday

Blood blossoms in the ring
as you fondle his face with leathered hands
like a farmer fists dirt searching
for the right time to plant the right seed
in exactly the right place: left jab slap,
snap and slap, right cross

left hook, uppercut swoosh,
then left snapslap and another
until his face is a cornucopia of colors:
lips plump and purple as plums
filled with so much fluid
they split down the middle

at your touch; cheeks bruised
brown like overripe peaches
that refused to fall
when they were supposed to;
his eyelids are spring figs flashing
purple, red, yellow and green.

His head a waterlogged cantaloupe
that almost looks human; strange fruit.
Someone should have stopped this already.
Cheers turning to jeers for the ref
to hold your hands from plowing

'cause the poor bastard can't see;
his eyeballs burrowed deep
like pits of grapefruits,

lids sutured shut by eyelashes:
The towel! someone shouts.
Where's the towel!

But you can't stop. You won't.
He's the blond boy
who made you notice a rainbow
has no black; he looks
like the stranger on the bus
who called your father that word,
that word, right in front of you.

You beat this man's face
into the flag of too many countries
because you still can't forget the loss
to Sugar Ray Leonard at the Olympic trials.
And you can't stop because
of why you started fighting:

that slow scratchy song about poplar trees
your mama played when you were too young
to ball fists big enough
so gloves wouldn't slip off
as you swung.

You do this for black bodies swinging
in faded grey photos, bulging eyes
and twisted mouths, fists fastened
behind so they couldn't fight back.

Tonight your farmer's fists furrow
sucker punch memories, determined
to forge your own rainbow, your flag
and glimmering gold medal
out of this man's fertile face.

THE RING

I'm scared every time I go into the ring, but it's how you handle it. What you have to do is plant your feet, bite down on your mouthpiece and say, "Let's go."

—Mike Tyson

What fighters fear most is losing
control of fists, their feet;
they fear the shape a face makes
when muscles stop working together.

It can happen anytime, without warning,
from just one punch in the wrong place
where blood buries bone and muscles
meet nerves deep beneath skin.

Boxers do their best to hide
these bloody circuit breakers
or run when another fighter finds
the secret spot that can make him swim
his hands as if he were drowning on land.

This is what fighters fear most:
losing control of lips so they pucker
and flap in the wind like a horse's hiccup
or an awkward boy trying to kiss a girl
for the first time.

Even a veteran will throw a fight
before he lets a wife see
his knees wobble and hands crawl
on air trying to hug another man
as if he were a secret lover.

I've seen a fighter take a fall
from a weak body shot because
it was the best excuse to take a knee
while he could still do it on his own.
Fans hate this.

But only boxers know
what hides between punches:
that lightning long second when you realize
bouncing spotlights overhead
really aren't moving,
flapping mouths of fans are silent

and the ring rope tangle
isn't a soft and warm bed sheet
but a sticky webtrap
from a giant spider
with too many arms.

I've seen all this and more:
the fright peeking white
from behind puffy slits and
swinging lips falling uncontrollably
like an elephant's trunk
over a crooked jaw

as the boxer bent over to grunt
a brown spot of wet shit
on white shorts
from another body shot
that made ringside novices giggle,

and the pro nearby squint
then jerk his head away
as if he were slipping a punch
and the realization
his fight was later that night
in this very same ring.

ARS POETICA

Meditation on *Boxer at Rest*, Greek Bronze, 50 BCE, attributed to
Lysippos

Art historians say you
may be Herakles, or perhaps
someone else with a cracked nose,
bruised eye, slit cheek, and cauliflower ears,
broken fists and forearms noosed
by oxhide straps. A man no one knows

with a jaw locked open for centuries
as if exhaling or inhaling
a question, exhortation, accusation...
Hair locks curling over themselves
again and again like roundhouse swings
or lactic acid routines
at the Lyceum

designed to merge form with function.
You would be Rodin's Thinker,
if not for thick shoulders,
biceps and forearms carved
into a sling shot at rest
but always ready.

Rigor mortis patin
the chronicle of a crime
that is confused for art
as you sit, just sit
on a crooked rock
because it hurts too much
to move.

IV.

GLADIATORS

You don't understand. I could have had class. I could have been a contender. I could have been somebody, instead of a bum—which is what I am.

—Marlon Brando, *On The Waterfront* (1954)

WORK

In 1979 a man could still find work
at the Houston Ship Channel
in oversized metal barns crowded
with five foot coils of steel cable
and wooden crates, foreign letters all over,
stacked on bricks to make bleachers.

They'd line up by five thirty or six
after day jobs that felt like training,
hoping to be picked
for a last-minute match up
if enough betters were in town
for a convention.

The first fight of the night
would be like all the rest:
both boxers sliding around each other
trying to look busy by grunting too loud
each time they missed.
They'd give it away by barely dancing,
just hopping sloppy weight,
one foot to the other,
back again, then again.

Neither man wants to be there.
One balding already, his U-shaped crown
sweating into a wreath of black feathers,
thin lines of grey in-between. Both
with bulges like someone's father
who doesn't bother to hide it anymore
because he's just too damn tired
from a full shift and
the sun all day.

They have forgotten
how long a three-minute round can be
when your hands are weighted down

like a metal lathe. This
will make it impossible to punch
and block your body and face
at the same time. One
will sacrifice his forehead;
the other a stomach.
This will count as strategy.

If they're lucky
they'll get home by midnight,
not too marked up
to make a wife mad
about another doctor bill.
One will have two twenties to offer.
The other ten for a bottle
to pass time 'til he gets picked
from the line up two weeks later
if his bus is running on time and
he can suck in his gut long enough to grunt
I'll take anything you got.

GLADIATOR

The lovely light of the moon's beautiful face lit up the evening and in the delightful festivities the whole precinct rang with a song in praise of victory.

—Pindar, *Odes*, 476 B.C.

Munera sine missione.
—Chant at Roman Gladiator Fights, circa 100 CE

He is always the first to fight those nights
fortunes are made on men not half as brave.
A perpetual opponent, he creeps into the cage
one crooked leg at a time, head cocked, eyes wide
with that ancient fear of being eaten alive.

He knows the crowd has paid to watch him sacrificed
but he'll punch and pull, mouth agape,
reminding us of a time when men flapped arms
so hard they would have flown into clouds
if not for the iron tied to their fists.

He knows he is too old for this, now, belly so big
he lets it do what it wants. His file red-flagged
ten years ago by the WBC doctor who feared
it would come to this: the journeyman.

He has never made more than fifty dollars a fight
but still finds that will, wicked and wild,
of an ancient martyr who steps to the gallows
with a smirk on his face even though he hears
the mob hate him.

He knows he will be carried out in buckets tonight,
but the hand-picked tattoo of his daughter's name
is enough to raise handcuffed hands and keep the legs
from running into stands. She will help him
throw a punch in-between head butts and bites.

For her he'll ignore crimson claw marks torn from his face
by padded paws of the animal in front of him; for her
he'll point the tip of his head forward like a sword,
charge and keep charging until his bluing body
betrays him and falls to the mat with the weight
of too many years of bad food and worse work.

But he will not quit. He will claw at rungs
of an invisible ladder until he falls face down again
and again in a ritual that makes the ring rattle like a bell
that'll start the crowd cheering for the winner
instead of this man, who always knew he would lose
but climbed into the ring anyway.

ODE TO THE BRONX EVERLAST
FACTORY, 1917-2003

No one can say who really won
the glory story contest
because everyone lies
about their record.

Someone said the new guy
on the canvas sewing rig
wasn't even a boxer,
much less Golden Gloves champ
of Brooklyn.

John the leather cutter
says he was an AAU referee there
and never saw him fight:
skinny dope fiend don't know shit
'bout boxing, and still owes me
ten bucks.

Everyone here has boxing ring fantasies
getting bigger and coming true
with each cut and stitch.
Even Big Mary in the front office says
she was a ring girl once.

Jerome the heavyweight champ of Ohio
just flashes toothless smile
and holds his sandwich overhead like a ring number
each time she walks to the Coke machine
at lunchtime.

But flat-faced Joey's the real thing:
he's a glove inspector and
tries every pair because his hands
were broken in the ring so many times
they fit like a fighter wrapped in gauze
for a title match.

No one dares say anything
as he punches himself
in the face like a pro
preparing for the worst
even though this isn't part
of the Everlast Quality Control Test.

He meets each glove with a headsmack
like two fighters tapping fists
before some far away fight
he tries to remember.
What was that fighter's name?
his lips seem to say,

banging his head over and over
into red leather gloves
until he feels the overhead lights again
burning his scalp like a garland,
the crowd parting

like a sea to let him pass
so he can climb the ring
where he'll hover
above the canvas on winged feet,
toes tucked tight into size six boxing boots

that could have been stitched
together in the next work bay
by two Puerto Rican girls
who swear their uncle
is three-time world champion Wilfredo Benitez.

When flat-faced Joey is done dreaming,
he'll stare down each glove
like a fighter trying too hard to seem fierce
before tossing them into a wheeled basket
he'll roll to the loading bay one last time
today at 5:00 p.m. where

everyone is planning to gather
for another round of stories
and sips of straight rot gut
from the bodega next door,
delaying as long as they can

their obligation to pull down the bay hatch
on their warehouse of dreams and
machines that have hummed, clapped
and screeched for eighty six years
like an arena full of fans.

SIGN OF THE CROSS

After scratchy mariachi trumpets
and rapid rap rhythms
rouse the crowd of bettors
to their feet, and

the hired baritone belches
rhymed stable names
that sound silly
and psychopathic, after

a bow-tied black man mouths
bland ring rules no one can hear
because everybody's heart
is thumping too loud: the stare down

and fake snarls that always fail
to hide a fighter's fright; after this
and a forced pat of gloves,
the admonition to *fight fair*
and protect yourself at all times,

borrowed white robes are released
because screams of *Ring the bell goddamit!*
are getting too loud to ignore.
This is when a Mexican fighter

will always take a knee
and make a quickly silent sign of the cross
as he looks down the padded canvas path
to the lion in front of him.

This will not be a prayer for victory
but a prayer nonetheless because
every boxer can be sure of only one thing:
he'll be carried out the ring

hands spread out
hailing his triumph, or
he'll be heaving and heavy
as they peel him off the tangle of ropes,

a crown of blood
and purple patches all over
that will have made the crowd go silent
for a moment, just a moment,
from shock and the shame
of having been witness to it all.

THE KID FROM MAGNOLIA

The sizzling insect buzz of neon lights
from a church basement or junior high gym
will have to do. The Amateur Athletic Union
doesn't have enough money and
won't sanction gypsy tournaments because
everyone knows what these coaches are like,
and the fans.

But we don't mind fighting off-circuit.
Everyone needs practice and they always find
a baritone to boar out nicknames
created on the spot: *Galena Park Gladiator;*
The Houston Hitman; Corpus Christi Killer.
Or he'll just call a fighter *The Kid*
from one neighborhood or another
if the reputation is bad enough.

You can get a hotdog for a dollar here,
popcorn is fifty cents and
it's not too hard to sneak a six pack
or take a swig from coach's whiskey bottle.
Someone will have an 8-Track of *Queen,*
maybe *Zeppelin* or *Saturday Night Fever*
even though disco is all wrong
for this place.

Some novices will still be stupid
enough to bring a sister
you can kiss under the stands
or finger behind a church pew
if the janitor got reckless with the lock,
WE ARE THE CHAMPIONS

thumping upstairs loud as sin,
making everyone anxious to climb the ring
and wind around another boy like moths
circling a bulb, each trying to trick the other
into getting close enough to fist him
into the flame and make his face sizzle,

while a swarm of boys whirlpool outside the ring,
counting down matches before their fights,
wondering what nickname they'll get,
silently praying it'll be fierce enough
to keep the other boy from face-painting him
with so much boxing ring rouge
he'll be called *chula* all night;

each silent pact with God
competing with the others
for your own ring name to get sung
under sizzling tubes that sometimes burst
like a photographer's flash
in a championship fight on live TV
that'll release the soprano wail of the crowd
so loud you'll raise the other hand, too,

as if trying to pull yourself to the rafters
so everyone can see it is you who won, you,
and not someone else, not the other guy
but *me, me, me,*
because deep down you know, you
just know this is as good
as its ever gonna get.

PASCAL'S WAGER

Let us weigh the gain and the loss in wagering that God is...If you gain, you gain all; if you lose, you lose nothing. Wager, then, without hesitation that He is.

—Blaise Pascal (1650)

It'll be fun to pull on a pair
of spongy gloves and play
punch with the boy next door.
You've fought before and know
you'll be friends again.

I'll be Ali, running around the ring
in a joke that makes us laugh
until the coach starts yelling:
Aim for the face!
The face! The face!

He's talking about you.
And even though you know
the fight isn't for real
you fist your friend back
everyday for a month

until you are too afraid
to tell him secrets
or ask for a taco
when your mom is drunk again
and forgot to cook.

After two months both
get so good with a gut punch
you learn to keep lungs empty
so the air doesn't get knocked out
by surprise.

You know better
than to breath in the ring.
In a year you will stop speaking.
Pros have more to teach

about counterpunch combo attacks
and you just can't understand
how a true friend can hit you
like that without saying a word
on the bus ride home.

It will take two years
of calculated uppercuts and
right crosses to move up in weight
with men who hit so hard
they make you look like a mystic,

pawing at starbursts behind eyes,
speaking strange tongues
like the blind preacher
in the Saturday night tent
on the corner of Wayside and Canal.

In five years coach will say
it's time to turn pro
because you're losing too many matches
for free and he's behind
on the light bill.

By then, you have learned
how to block out the urge to hug
when you're hurt; you can ignore
screaming drunks mad you didn't fall
when they bet you would.

At twenty you will know for sure
a boxing coach can't teach enough
to keep you safe from dark demons
hiding behind red leather gloves,

casting spells that make you float
on your feet as the woofers
in your head burst into silence.
By your first pro fight

you are no longer the boy
who wriggled hands into a pair of gloves
with the satisfaction a novice priest feels
as he slips into a frock the first time.
You know the truth, the whole truth,

but you will take a chance anyway because
you know you must face the beast alone,
everyday, and you've got nothing
to lose, nothing at all, by saying a prayer
before the bell rings.

MAN TO MAN
For Benny "The Kid" Paret
born in Santa Clara, Cuba March 14, 1937,
killed in the Welterweight Championship with Emile Griffith, April 3, 1962

I keep thinking how strange it is...I kill a man and most people
understand and forgive me...However, I love a man, and to so many
people this is an unforgivable sin; it makes me an evil person. So, even
though I never went to jail, I have been in prison almost all my life.

—Emile Griffith, Former Welterweight, Middleweight
and Junior Middleweight World Champion

Boxing is blood, tart-tasting blood
bonded with salt sweat into a lubricant
that keeps you from getting a good hold
of the man who has been trying all night
to paint your face pink, red and purple
as if you were his lover. Boxing

makes enemies of two men
who spent seven months staring
at muscles in the gym, wondering
at their strength, how hard
they can become, if the bicep
and flexed forearm will be strong enough
to lift you in a clinch, turn you around
against the ropes so hard the ring
will squeak like bedsprings.

This is boxing: two men barely clothed,
sweaty with saliva jaws, huffing
like battling bulls who have forgotten the plump cows
standing by, ready, waiting, wondering
if this will ever end. Boxing
is Emile Griffith fisting Benny Paret
for calling him *maricón* at the weigh-in
until he lay splayed on his stomach
plump ass up.

It is the overripe apricot smell
of shit from a gut punch fart, the sticky wet
splatter of a headbutt greased with Vaseline
that keeps you connected by a long glob
of glimmering goo as you try to pull away
to plant your feet in a new position
for the next thrust. Boxing

hurts like sex, the inside-out tingle
from a million pin prick spasms
along lower spine, sphincter, *ombligo*;
thigh muscles flexed firm. A perfect punch

will make the other man moan
as if it felt good; grunting to catch his breath
until it is his turn to plant hooves, push
the blood up from foot to hamstring, butt
and backbone into a right hand counterpunch,
his swollen red leather bulb ready to explode
as soon as it touches flesh.

PRETTYBOY

He doesn't belong here but doesn't know yet
because he hasn't been hit by a hungry fighter
who makes meals by cracking white skullshells
and scrambling yellow pulp inside.
He's a *Prettyboy*. Every gym has one:

the well-built welterweight who was a model once
but now spends five days a week watching himself
shadow box in the full-bodied mirror
coach Jim hung to cover cracks
from plumbing pulled out last year.

No one uses it but him. That's why we call him
Prettyboy. He pauses between slow motion combos
with a runway turn and nod down at bicep
he makes rise with a short grunt that makes us laugh
because it looks like he's forcing out a fart.

Coach Jim hasn't said anything. He hopes *Prettyboy*
will buy boxing trunks for the amateurs
like the ones he wears: black satin
with thick gold side stripes shimmering like sweat.

Even the white pros call him *stupid whiteboy*.
He pretends not to hear this and
that Mexican amateur who shakes his head
slowly pronouncing each syllable of *Pu-*
Ta! loud enough for everyone to hear.

The sexy sound when he says *I'm a boxer*
keeps him coming back every day for five weeks;
he loves the faceshock of disco queens at the club
who spread their eyes wide when he explains
how tough it is in the gym.

You can tell he eats well by his full cheeks.
He came to the gym in a suit once. This
is why no one wants to work with him,
all silent to his well-pronounced *Hello gentlemen*...

Everyone drawing lots with their stares
to get in the ring with him and
feed a real fighter's appetite for face soup,
over easy eyes and sticky ground up *lengua*
only poor people have learned to eat
because they never had a choice.

THE DOCKS

After arms could no longer paddle
thick sweaty soups of mist
thrown up by screaming leather mitts,
heavy bag grunts and speed bag shuffle
that looked like water-logged remains
of a crime victim bobbing back and forth,
back and forth in a wild wicked sea,
it was time to work the legs. Outside

the curb crumbled into more
crumbled concrete from Clinton Drive
to wooden docks where cargo was loaded
and unloaded in sacks, like us,
one hundred pounds at a time,
by sweaty wet black men and brown men
who were boxers once, and
full of dreams, too.

We pumped legs like fists, fast
flexing muscles barely strong enough
to carry a flyweight. We fought
each other with feet, feeling our way
through potholes, slapping at puddles,
trying to outrun cracks creaking past
silos and metal-framed warehouses
wheezing in the ship-channel mist
because everyone was out of breath,
and everything. We pumped

with all that was left of the arms,
racing each other and those putrid acids
growing in our veins that could freeze
limbs solid if we didn't pace ourselves.
We pushed harder than we should have
because this was our field of dreams;
the crowd of longshoremen cheering
our daily return like ritual

as if we were ancient warriors
returning from battle: a cotton-striped work hat
thrown up like a wreath; fists pumped high
by another man who bet a round of beers
on the skinny dark one in front; hollers
and whistles and hoorahs like you see
in the Olympics on TV. We
were champions, their champions,

and they cheered barrel-chested roars
with flexed arm muscles cracking into road maps
or big bulging sea lane swells
to foreign ports that rows and rows
of ten-story cargo ships would load
and unload, one hundred pounds at a time,

the rainbow of foreign flags fluttering in ceremony
as we ran cracked crooked streets to the docks
every afternoon before the sun went down.

CATFIGHT

For Mia "The Knockout" St. John Rosales
1999 Playboy Playmate
2005 International Female Boxing Association Lightweight Champion

> *Raw aggression is thought to be the peculiar province of men, as nurturing is the peculiar province of women. (The female boxer violates this stereotype and cannot be taken seriously—she is parody, she is cartoon, she is monstrous. Had she an ideology, she is likely to be a feminist.)*
>
> —Joyce Carol Oates, *On Boxing* (1987)

The crowd always gave it away:
prepubescent boys pawing
and pulling over shoulders like crabs
meant this was a catfight,
those schoolyard riots at Franklin Elementary
that fed our curiosities.

You never knew what you'd get.
Sometimes just a shirt sleeve
shorn off the girl a friend swears
made-out with her guy, or
splatter of blood pulled from the nose
of a preteen who called the other girl *bitch*
behind her back.

A blouse was the biggest trophy;
a boy would blacken your eye
to get a sliver he would later trade
for a cookie at lunchtime.
It was every girl's fear
her frilly top would give way or worse:
the Wonder Woman bra grandma bought
might burst and all would see
her nubby mounds.

Taunts would force the loser
to leave school, so both swung
rotary blades, polish-hardened claws

flung out like the two-headed beast
they had become; anything
to avoid crumpling like dirty laundry
for scavengers to pick;

each girl gripping tight
like cats too far on a limb
until one emerged from the lump
of balled bodies, a shard of shirt
or clump of hairy scalp, barrettes
still attached, hiccupping a teary victory
with Medusa's bloody mange at her side

to the cheers and jeers of *Hit her tits!*
Punch her pussy! Kiss her puta!
she'd hear years later in the ring
surrounded by boys much older now
who paid good money to see this again.

POUND FOR POUND

A pro will finger and flip every crisp page
of *Ring Magazine* like a chronic gambler
headchasing eyeballs across each line
of a trackbook, adding, subtracting

a horse's weight, age, number of races
trying to calculate the value
of frantic hoofbeats and
stinging jockey whipslaps
you can hear all the way to the cheap seats.

Rank means everything in boxing.
This is why a fighter will shout *Bullshit!*
to the monthly tally of a sportswriter
who claims to know the best fighter
pound for pound in the world
without ever stepping into the ring.

A pro knows that speed, weight and
fate can't be quantified. But
he'll still put faith in a coach
who claims to know the slave master's calculus
of hunger and pain to maximize a man's strength
at the lowest possible weight.

A fighter will do anything for just a line-
long mention in *Ring Magazine*:
force a vomit everyday for a month
or spit in a coke can all morning to make weight.
His pay depends on him
getting every single number just right.

Every boxer has a series of numbers:
Age. Fights. Rank. Reach. Weight.
Weight means everything in boxing.
Heavyweights are 190 pounds or more.
A Featherweight will be 122-126.

A true Bantamweight weighs
between 118 and 122 pounds.
The four pound range can make
the difference between a horsequick start
or sluggish finish with a nose flattened
and too bruised to break the finish line tape.

This is the fiercest division in boxing
with more pound-for-pound greats
than any other. The name says it all:
Bantamweight means rooster in Spanish.
Gallo: a Mexican fighting cock bred just right

and trained to flutter through a hurricane
of feathers, spurs burned onto feet
flung out kicking, kicking, kicking
into another beast's bloody red breast
even after its own heart stops beating.

The Superflyweight is next
at 115-118. A true Flyweight
can't weigh less than 112 pounds
and never more than 115.
They're quick as airborne insects
but can't hit worth a shit. No power.

Light as a jockey; small
as a prepubescent boy too young
to realize everyone around him is a beast
trying to splay him down and feast
on his tiny tasty flesh.

The lowest division is Strawweight.
Under 105 pounds. Always. Lighter
than a rooster's feather or a fly. Strawweights
are grown men who look like full-formed elves.
They scan the pages of *Ring Magazine*, too,

trying to figure out if four generations
of malnourishment will finally pay off.
Their eyes magically quick and feet and fists, too,
but none powerful enough
to spin the strands into gold.

MY TÍA LUCY HATES BOXING

I.

My *Tía* Lucy turns away from the fight
on TV, nose wrinkled up, eyes tight
as if she could smell the stinky hot sweat
a boxer makes when he is trapped.
She knows what will happen next.

She's from a family of fighters
whose arms were never strong enough
to make them anything more
than working class. Tyrants
at home, all of them,

because after a full day of taking orders at work
they felt like they were in the gym again,
preparing for the big break
that only became a series of low-bet brawls
year after year after year
until they had no more bones
to bet.

They were proud bone breakers, once.
Now all they do is break things, anything,
Women in the family sweep
up broken plates. Pick up chairs.
But fistprint fossils still crawl
across newly painted drywall.

II.

She hates boxing, my *Tía* Lucy,
because it never brought men
in the family anything.
Nothing.

All she got was a husband
and brother-in-law who punch fists all day
into electrified vats at the plating shop
making shiny chrome bumpers and
trinkets of gold.

It gave her a brother
who became famous all over town
only to weigh down his golden arm
with bottle caps of boiling brown liquid.
He could have been a contender
if not for prison.

Another brother's back bent
like pipes he fondled at the factory
everyday until the foreman told him
to just stop coming because
his hands had become too slow
to keep up with young bucks
begging for work each morning.

With no more opponents
he couldn't see the bottle
hit him from behind
like a rabbit punch.

III.

My *Tía* Lucy turns away
from the fight on TV.
She just can't stand to see
a man broken like that
in front of everyone.
She's seen it all before:

a man's face crunched stupid, eyes crossed
and glazed like a newlywed,
lips pursed crooked as if he were drunk
with too much champagne from the reception,
begging for a kiss
from an angry new wife.

She just shakes her head.
She knows what's behind
a winner's smile: he's just a boy
trying to make an absent father proud,
and he's surprised, too, that he won,
wondering how long he can hide
behind the muscles of a raised right hand,

the man on the ground a reminder
of what awaits all boxers
after the lights and shouts and
gold-plated belts
manufactured by workers
who once had their own hands raised high
in victory.

My *Tía* Lucy has seen all this before
and she hates it, she just hates it all.

TWIST

It's all in the hips, twisting hip joint jaunts
turning your torso like a ballroom dancer
to dodge a grocery cart loaded
with lettuce and oranges that cost
forty nine cents a pound today.
No. Really. It's okay.
But she apologizes again
and again with crunched eyebrows
because she just doesn't know
how well you slipped the silver metal jab
without even trying.

It's always like that; hips twisting
and turning on their own
when you least expect it
and in all the wrong places:
the Eucharist line at church
when the priest tries to punch you
in the mouth; a classroom of students
with hands raised high like a flurry of jabs;
the cash register where a teenager tries
to hit you in the chest with his fist
full of change. You twist. Twitch.
Can't help from twitching all the time.
It's the training: years

of bobbing and weaving
under a clothesline that's hunched you over
before you were twenty; the crouch-twist-punch routine
that saved you from corner rope traps
too many times to count;
coach Jim's wet towel slaps to the torso
that stung a red welt if you didn't twist in time;
dance steps—rounds and rounds of hopping and
sliding back and forth and to the sides...
It would have been beautiful
if not for all the pain. Yes,

it's the training. The hips give it away.
But you can't help it; you just never know
if the outstretched hand of a friend
will conceal a right cross
or upper cut to the chin.
The body can't help but twitch
when someone gets in range
'cause this means you're in range, too.
It twists all the time, like it's supposed to
when a careless child bumps behind
or a parent crowds you at the register.
The training was meant to last,
and the beatings, too. So your body twists
and twists and twists...

At forty all you can do is hope
the hips will give up some day soon
so you can get to your grocery list.
Oranges are forty-nine cents a pound today,
and avocados a dollar each.
But you don't dare. You're afraid
if you stretch forward with fists
to feel for the good ones
your hips will run off again
because this place is too crowded on Sundays
and you just never know
if those grenade-shaped fruit shells
will explode at your touch.

V.
ODE TO ALI

Me. Weeeee…

—Muhammad Ali (1963)

ODE TO ALI

Ain't no such thing as a boxing poet,
'cept of course Ali. Muhammad Ali.
He could bust a rhyme while keeping time
with shuffling feet and flying fists
that set typewriters clacking
and people clapping
from Kentucky to Kinsasha: *Ali Bumbayé!*

He was a beautiful man
in a brutal time
when Africans in America
were given *nigger* for a name.
But this Black Man wouldn't
Step-n-fetch-it 'cause Ali
didn't take shit from nobody!

In another skin and another time
he'd be a salon poet reciting rhymes
about the simplicity of the human mind
and miracle of a blade of grass.
His hands would be soft and pink
instead of scarred plump dumbbells
used to tabulate the worth
of a man at auction
on the Las Vegas boxing circuit.
His fists an abacus of anger
clicking and clacking over
and over again: *Ain't Nobody's Nigga!*
NOOOOOOBODY'S NIGGA!

Ali was a sweet man, a sweet man
child who grew up with fists
for toys. But he knew how to share.
He shared all he had
with any who asked
'cause Ali was just like that, generous
as a poet who offers a rhyme

to help us pass the time
after beatings at work, home
and everyplace in between.

Ali knew. He knew
what that was like,
so he gave us a smile
even though it left him open
to a right cross that twisted his face stupid.
But Ali didn't let a simple beating
beat him. He made a song
of the slapping and whistling wind
from other punches he made miss;
he'd move, mock and rock to help
us smile, too, laugh with him.

He invited us to a dance
in the middle of the ring
and shout at the top of his lungs
I AM THE GREATEST!
THEEE GREAAAATEST!
A gift of gauche from a man
who talked like all our fathers
were afraid to talk except
when they were drunk
or beating a woman.

Ali, Muhammad Ali, the man
was a poet I tell you,
a poet who could bust a rhyme
while keeping time with whistling
combinations, one-two, left-right,
triple left, right, down then up
and down again for the next measure;
Ali was a conductor who knew
how to use his hands to make music.

He could command trumpets
and bassoons to call for war,
set the violin section running
like a cavalry with swords
drawn, he'd command the trombones
and tubas to honor the fallen,
call flutes, clarinets and cymbals
to ring like a poem: MUSIC!
And he could sing, too.

Today, Ali can barely speak in splatters
and slurs because in those days
everyone wanted to be famous for
an hour so they skipped, smacked
and cracked the bones of his face
and forehead, sent his brain
bubbling back and forth
in a pool of burst blood vessels.

Angry, they were angry
because they knew
they were just fighters
not poets like Ali.
They hated him,
despised the butterflies and
bees he set loose
because everybody knows
there ain't no such thing
as a goddamned boxing poet,

'cept of course Ali,
Muhammad Ali,
a warrior who knew
how to sing a song
with slips and slaps
of the padded batons
that sent the crowd dancing

in their seats like amateurs
do before their first fight.

And he fought
by refusing to fight
what wasn't right:
No Viet Cong ever called me nigger
This war's wrong!
he said in a song.
Only Ali could rant and rhyme
at the same time. He gave us this
because he knew we could not
go on without.
He took a beating for it,
our beating.

He took beatings because
we asked him to sing for us,
to dance one more time
even after his voice went hoarse
and body bent and bloated
with age and other men's rage.
He took beatings, too many
beatings, to mark time
when he could no longer sing
his songs because he knew
we needed him
to explain the beauty
of our blackness
and all the colors of the rainbow.
We needed his music, his
manhood. Muhammad Ali.
Yes, Muhammad Ali, he
was a poet...

GLOSSARY

AAU. The Amateur Athletic Union governs amateur boxing in the U.S. and internationally.

Ali Bumbayé. The chant that Muhammad Ali's fans shouted in Kinshasa, Zaire in 1974, roughly translated as "Ali Kill Him."

Bantamweight. A weight division in boxing that consists of fighters between 118-122 pounds. In Spanish this term translates as *Gallo*, which is a rooster, or fighting cock.

Barrio. Working class Mexican American or Latino neighborhood.

Bellum omnium contra omnes. Latin for *war of one against all*, which Thomas Hobbes proposed as the primal human condition in *Leviathan* (1651).

Boe-lahs. Phonetic spelling of *bolas*, which is a vernacular Anglicized Spanish term for *balls*.

Chinga tu madre. A common Spanish vernacular insult that roughly translates as *fuck your mother*.

Chula. Spanish for *pretty girl*.

El Cucuí. Spanish for *Boogeyman*.

Featherweight. A weight division in boxing that consists of fighters between 126-130 pounds.

Fideo. Mexican dish made with noodles, pork, and a light tomato base.

Flyweight. A weight division in boxing that consists of fighters between 108-112 pounds.

Galena Park. Working class suburb east of Houston, Texas adjacent to the docks of the eastern shore of the Houston Ship Channel.

Gallo. Spanish for rooster and also refers to the *Bantamweight* division in boxing

Grito. Spanish for *shout*, usually offered in celebration, but also to taunt someone or to express anger.

El Huracán del norte. Spanish for *Hurricane of the North*, the ring name used by my uncle Basilio Ruiz.

IFBA. The IFBA, or International Female Boxing Association, is one of several regulatory agencies governing female boxing.

Lengua. Inexpensive Mexican delicacy made of boiled cow
    tongue.
Lightweight. A weight division in boxing that consists of fighters
    weighing 135-140 pounds.
Madrina. Spanish for *Godmother,* usually someone close to the
    immediate family who sponsors a child during their
    Catholic rites of First Communion and Confirmation.
Magnolia. Working class barrio in southeast Houston, Texas that
    abuts the western shore of the Houston Ship Channel.
Manteca. Lard used in *pan dulce,* Mexican sweet bread.
Maracas. A Caribbean musical instrument made by filling a dried
    gourd with small pebbles to make a rattle.
Maricón. Spanish vernacular epithet for a homosexual that
    translates as *fag.*
Mayate. Spanish epithet for Black person that roughly translates
    as *nigger.*
Munera sine missione. Latin phrase for gladiator fights that loosely
    translates as *contest without end,* or more practically, *fight
    to the death.*
The Olympiad. Renowned boxing gym and tournament venue in
    downtown Houston, Texas that operated into the late
    1980s before the building was demolished.
Omligo. Spanish for belly button.
Pan dulce. Spanish for *sweet bread,* a Mexican delicacy that
    consists of a variety of sugar coated breads, cookies and
    filled pastries.
Pinche. Vernacular Spanish modifier that roughly translates as
    damned.
Puta. Spanish vernacular epithet that translates as *bitch.*
Sam Houston Coliseum. Sports arena in downtown Houston,
    Texas, that was host to wrestling and boxing matches
    until the 1990s, when it was converted into a multiplex
    cinema.
Tía and *Tío.* Spanish for *aunt* and *uncle.*
Verga. Spanish vernacular for dick.
y pa' mis tíos Valdez. Spanish phrase that translates *and for my
    Valdez uncles.*

BOXING WEIGHT DIVISIONS

Straw Weight – 48 kg. /105 lbs.

Mini Flyweight – 48 kg. /105 lbs.

Junior Flyweight – 49 kg. /108 lbs.

Light Flyweight – 49 kg. / 108 lbs.

Flyweight – 51 kg. / 112 lbs.

Junior Bantam – 52 kg. / 115 lbs.

Super Flyweight – 52 kg. / 115 lbs.

Bantamweight – 54 kg. / 118 lbs.

Junior Featherweight – 55 kg. / 122 lbs.

Super Bantamweight – 55 kg. / 122 lbs.

Featherweight – 57 kg. / 126 lbs.

Junior Lightweight – 59 kg. / 130 lbs.

Super Featherweight – 59 kg. / 130 lbs.

Lightweight – 61 kg. / 135 lbs.

Junior Welterweight – 65 kg. / 140 lbs.

Super lightweight – 65 kg. / 140 lbs.

Welterweight – 67 kg. / 147 lbs.

Junior Middleweight – 70 kg. / 154 lbs.

Super Welterweight – 70 kg. / 154 lbs.

Middleweight – 73 kg. / 160 lbs.

Super Middleweight – 76 kg. / 168 lbs.

Light Heavyweight – 79 kg. / 175 lbs.

Cruiserweight – 86 kg. / 190 lbs.

Heavyweight – 86+ kg. / 190+ lbs.

ABOUT THE AUTHOR

B.V. OLGUÍN was born in 1965 and raised in a working class barrio in the lower east side of Houston, Texas, known as Magnolia. He was an undefeated amateur boxer (14-0, 2 KO), and has worked as a unionized grocery worker, construction worker, prison educator, university professor, volunteer Emergency Medical Technician, and also is a member of the *Venceremos* Brigade. He received a B.A. from the University of Houston in 1989, where his maternal grandfather worked as a janitor, and an M.A. and Ph.D. from Stanford University in 1992 and 1996, respectively.

Olguín is a member of the Macondo Writers Workshop founded by Sandra Cisneros, and is the author of a second collection of poetry, *At the Risk of Seeming Ridiculous*, and currently working on a third, *Pericardial Tamponade*. Olguín's poetry has been published in journals such as *Borderlands, Callaloo, North American Review*, and elsewhere. His jointly-authored translation of Américo Paredes's 1937 collection of poetry, *Cantos de Adolescencia/Songs of Youth*, was published by Arte Público Press in 2007, and received the International Latino Book Award in 2008. He also is the author of a research manuscript, *La Pinta: Chicana/o Prisoner Literature, Culture and Politics* (University of Texas Press, 2010), and a forthcoming book on war literature.

B.V. Olguín currently is an Associate Professor of Literature and Creative Writing in the English Department at the University of Texas at San Antonio.

CPSIA information can be obtained at www.ICGtesting.com
Printed in the USA
BVOW03s1930041114

373529BV00006B/9/P